For Mexico, amazing country full of everything.

Always hard the day before
what do I pack
(emergency bagel)
what do I leave
(every single necklace)
what books will I want in Mexico
(download many)
how many notebooks
how many earrings
of course there is absolutely everything
there earrings books
what do we want from this vacation
finally on the road to somewhere else
to leave a part of ourselves behind
(The day before,
I bought an ugly grey nylon bag
with many zippers thinking
at last I will be organized,
brought it home and Peter said
you'll never carry that.
He was right.)

We flew to Houston
found Alchemy Cocktail bar
talked with people from Milwaukee
who'd gone to Oaxaca four times
woman from Canada who described
her many pickleball games
two identical brothers Don and Tom
from southern Nebraska
wearing identical My Evil Twin t-shirts
on their way, for the very first time
to Oaxaca intending to drink Mezcal.
When you travel what you see
is everything all over again.
Diego waiter on the roof
of our hotel wants to be
a mixologist.
He practices drinks on me
his happy customer.
We walk and walk, stopping to look
at more or less everything:
continual celebrations,
street vendors selling fried caterpillars,
jugglers, children,
two weddings back to back.

I know this is a place I could stay.
Rodrigo took four of us
on a car trip to a market
about an hour
outside of town where we
wandered looking looking
at so much made by hand.
Driving home we went to
a small rug village.
Beautiful young woman showed
us how she's raising silk
worms, making silk
thread by thread.
Her colors come
come from natural dyes:
pecan shells and cochineal,
pomegranates, marigold, and, moss
insects fly into cactus leaves,
then are removed by hand and squeezed
to reveal bright red, indigo, deep purple, orange.
Miracle of color and craft.
As we left we saw that she'd washed
her daughters' socks,
then elegantly dried them one by one

on the chain link fence outside.
One of the many books
I'd still like to write:
series called Don't Miss This
> about people and places I love.
> Oaxaca now.
> I suppose I'd have
> to include a few facts:
>> 18 ethnic groups
>> 10,523 tribal villages
>> eight regions in the province
>> but that would not be
>>> the subject of the poems
>>> (except this one.)
>>> I'd show you the people,
>>> their beautiful logos
>>> of course all the food.

Yesterday we walked.
Churches then lunch
search for an envelope
to mail our New York rent.
Everyone told us
don't mail letters from Mexico.
The post office was actually empty.
I'd made a dinner
reservation at a formal
place with a famous chef
but we canceled it and went
instead to a simple rooftop nearby.
Everyone in the streets
is walking somewhere.
Music on each corner.
Maria our waitress
said our food would make us happy
She was right.

This morning we are flying
to Mexico City -this morning
we are leaving a place
we've loved for seven days
people we loved too
to a big big city and although
I do love cities have lived
in one forever although I know
we will be staying
in a hotel with a very good bar
staying in a neighborhood
full of food and art
and people on the street
Oaxaca is a place
like Essaouira and Hanoi
where I looked at apartments
online thought maybe
that's where I should live.

Our new friend Amy
we will see her forever
has been coming to Oaxaca
for 60 years.
She knows many many people
in villages nearby. Yesterday
she took us with Rodrigo driving
to their houses to see their crafts:
handprinted mirrors, elaborate trunks,
dishes and pots the colors of earth.
Every house is full of color.
Leaving Oaxaca
will be hard. Today's
our last before Mexico City.
I'm sure that
we'll be back.

On our way to Mexico City
we met a Canadian nurse
who told us that she's traveled
to 60 countries. One of her trips
was a seven month sail
in a small boat from England
to Israel with Jewish doctor
who was her fiance
By the time they'd gotten to Israel
they broke up. She married
his friend. He married
an Israeli linguist. I hope
she doesn't go on a boat trip
with him she said.

In Mexico City we are staying
in Camino Real, spectacular.
Built for the Olympics
by Ricardo Legorreta. Oddly
it was the same price
as our funky unusual
Oaxacan hotel room.
The hotel is all colors and shapes.
Bright pink bright yellow bright blue.
We did not drink their blue martini.

When tourists visit New York
they go to MOMA and the MET
but what you see when you visit
somewhere is not the same
for all of us. We are in Polanco
Paul from Houston, a doorman
married a Mexican woman
he met on vacation.
They have three kids here.
Sergio, the other doorman
was born in San Miguel. They both told us
separately that we
are in a Jewish neighborhood now.
It's safe said Paul.
I look for Jews on these streets
but so far none.

At Pulpo restaurant
last night in a pleasant alleyway
in Roma (more hipster
than Polanco and probably
fewer Jews) owner Leslie
came to say hello. Lebanese,
she told us that there are many
Lebanese ex-pats here
(second to Brazil)
She gave us names
of her favorite Mexican Lebanese restaurants.
Her grandmother's Armenian,
And her food was delicious.

Arturo, our cab driver, spoke
better English than my Spanish
(easy to do). He is in medical school
studying to be
a gastroenterologist. Arturo was
happy to hear I have one.
Is your condition idiopathic
he asked. We were impressed
with his word. (I told him yes.)

Yesterday our driver
told us that his two brothers
have lived in Chicago
undocumented for 23 years.
They've only seen one another
on zoom. One brother has a son
in Mexico City who is 25 now.
The religious money changer's
store is called Ha Shem (God).
Our hotel is between
Emmanuel Kant, Leibniz, and Darwin Streets.
Claudia Sheinbaum Pardo
is the progressive Jewish mayor of Mexico City.
She will run for President.
Today we will meet
Khanyi's friend Aldara.
She lives nearby and will take
us for good tacos.
And tonight we will drink
margaritas, again.

Yesterday two beautiful sisters
Aldara and Romina
drove us around to see what they know.
Friends of our granddaughter
Khanyisile Ndaba
they all met about six years ago
at North Country camp.
A place becomes different
when someone who lives there
someone who knows it
explains. The sisters are both
in college now studying design.
They have a chartreuse car.
We went to Roma, their favorite
neighborhood, a little like
the old West Village. We walked
and walked and walked,
and they told us stories
about their families and their lives.
A place is always people
and if you're lucky you
somehow meet them.

We love what we can see
though what we understand
just passing through is not much.
None of our cab drivers
like the president like the mayor.
They all describe corruption.
Most drivers live
an hour and a half away.
Just walking around is wonderful.
So is the coffee, the chocolate, the food.
I bought orange and yellow
shoelaces from an old man
who cut them himself. He said I should
buy green too so I did.
Art Fair is here, an international
festival. Yesterday we went
to the gallery neighborhood
of San Miguel (Luis Barragan's
house is a museum there.)
and met an artist named BLKSMTH
from Portland, Oregon
who's part of the fair. He makes
large pink letters into words.
The words exist for an hour or two.

Museo Soumaya, Carlos Slim's
enormous collection is housed
in a disconcerting
building that belongs right here.
Many Rodins are reproductions.
Good Lebanese dinner and then,
our pink and orange and blue hotel.
This city is one place where we
will return before long.

What we learned:
We love this city for the energy
for the art
and for so much food.
Wonderful croissants everywhere
in Mexico City. Who knew?
Carlos Slim is not the richest
man in the world any more.
He's either fourth or eleventh.
His family are Maronite Christians
from Lebanon. He's both bad and good.
Art is a big value here.
And architecture and wonderful
graphic design. So many good numbers.
People are generally
skeptical of government.
They don't believe there can be
Mexican government without corruption.
They don't speak well
of any politicians.
Still, Mexicans seem kind and optimistic.
Last night we ate dinner
near the hotel at a restaurant
called Shakespeare 92.

The actual address. A restaurant valet
sat on a stool on the corner.
No one arrived in a car.
Mostly what we did in Mexico
was walk. Knowing
it's impossible
to understand what you see.
Before long we will try here again.

Our last day we walked
around the zocalo
wholesale neighborhoods
of ribbons, beads and embroidering
supplies: pictures and thread.
Men and women sit outside
embroidering. We walked to an
old cafeteria for cookies and coffee
walked and walked and walked
In our hotel my old yoga teacher Richard
with his wife and her sister
Hope and Charity.
We took an Uber to Merotoro
restaurant on a street that was an
old horsing track
to meet Laura's friend Rudy
who lives here now. (Rudy
and other friends recommended Merotoro
and now I'm recommending it for you.)
We spent hours talking with Rudy
about who he was who we are
and why we all love Mexico.

What we see and what we say
an infinite exercise.
We got a ride with Jose Luis
gentle driver from Mexican suburbs
his brothers undocumented
workers in Chicago for 23 years.
He doesn't like socialists
doesn't like immigrants.
He wants more rules.
Then San Miguel beautiful bubble
the kind of bubble we're happy to be
winding cobblestones
deep red houses
our apartment has a rooftop
people who paint
who write novels and poems
writers festivals all the time
Margaret Atwood reading Monday
a little Woodstock said our therapist neighbor
she's from Accord, New York
a little San Francisco says our
wonderful landlord she has commuted
from California to San Miguel for 33 years.
We meet good friends from home

last night for dinner with three new strangers.
Today we'll hear Mexican music in a campo nearby.
What is real and what is not.
How do you, when you go someplace that isn't yours,
how do you see and what do you understand.

Maxine took us in her car
to a concert in the campo
to a place owned by
Rebecca and Gil.
Forty five years ago
a boy named Gil
was playing music
on the street in Oaxaca
Doc Severinsen
from the Johnny Carson show
heard him play
brought him to LA
long long story
Gil married Rebecca
an LA Jewish woman
their sons went to NYU
now they're in San Miguel
with a music tent
in the campo. Maxine
took us there where we joined
a large happy group
of many people some even older
than we are who still
can dance.

Catholic woman we met
in San Miguel she is 80
entirely beautiful still
divorced a while
with four grown sons
told us that when she
was growing up in Indiana
she fell in love
with an Orthodox Jew
one of five boys
he asked her to marry
him and she said no.
His family would be trouble.
Sixty five years later
he is still in Indiana.
His wife is sick
they still have lunch
only lunch
twice a year.
Maybe now
she said.

San Miguel de Allende
heritage town absolutely gorgeous
houses weather cobble stone streets
some people say it's gentrified
too many people speaking English
not what it once was
not real not worth visiting
not as good as other places
say Oaxaca.
We saw good friends
made new ones
lived in an Airbnb with a rooftop terrace
ate many almond croissants
drank countless margaritas
glasses of hibiscus water
went dancing in the campo
lived in the bubble that a good vacation
can be when sky is all there is
and sun. And you're surrounded
by colors you didn't quite know before.

Crashed airport eggs
Odd menu word for a pre plane flight
Took me a minute
To know they meant scrambled.
For our last night
We drank at Deborah Turbeville fantastic
Old house. Now a hotel called
Casa No Name. One couple
In the bar. Handsome. Well dressed.
Their conversation in English
Entirely weather. (variations of
Colder stateside.)
Angel checked us in
at the Leon airport. No line.
I'm waiting for you to return he said.
I'm waiting too.

Easy trip from Leon to Houston
then so many people
we missed our flight.
United put us on an hour later
bumped to first class
we spent the flight
drinking champagne, eating hot pretzels
but first class cheese board dinner,
talking to our stewardess Leontine.
Her father green eyed Creole from New Orleans
went to work in a Colorado factory.
Mother at 16 took the train by herself
from Mexico to Colorado
got a job in the factory couldn't speak English
harassed by other employees.
Father came to her rescue they fell in love
learned each other's languages
had three daughters. Leontine herself
married three times
three children 11 grandchildren
22 great grandchildren so far.
A man friend now.
When I bring dessert
I'll tell you the rest
she said.

Mexico was wonderful
(there is no BUT)
and now we are home
in our full orange apartment
replete with years of flea markets
and life. First day home
the flea market across the street
was open
and even though I need
absolutely nothing
have some new Mexican
bottle cap refrigerator magnets
hand painted inside
gorgeous plastic striped bags
my favorite Oaxacan earrings
same ones I bought 20 years ago
lost one maybe 8 years ago
even though I need
Absolutely Nothing I went
across the street and found a purple
velvet robe in perfect condition.
If I took out the Gap label I could
probably get another ten dollars

said my friend Ruth who sold it to me.
She found a Goodwill by the pound
in Florida last week she even
bought two Dolce Gabbana dresses
then I got two rolls from the roll guy
my favorite watermelon radishes
we had brunch on the coffee table
with Peter's lattes
and although we aren't in Mexico
any more back on the brown
leather couch still we are
in New York City
full of people
and everything.

www.ingramcontent.com/pod-product-compliance
Lightning Source LLC
Chambersburg PA
CBHW030459010526
44118CB00011B/1017